CARING FOR THE PLANET
TEMPERATE WOODLANDS

Neil Champion

A⁺
Smart Apple Media

Published by Smart Apple Media
2140 Howard Drive West, North Mankato, MN 56003

Design and production by Helen James

Photographs by Alamy (adrian arbib, Bill Bachman, Juniors Bildarchiv,
blickwinkel, David Hoffman Photo Library, Danita Delimont, Dinodia
Images, Chad Ehlers, eye35.com, neil hardwick, Holt Studios International Ltd,
Nigel Hicks, Chris Howes / Wild Places Photography, Andre Jenny, Tina Manley,
Lauri Nykopp, Michael Patrick O'Neill, Edward Parker, Troy and Mary Parlee,
Photo Japan, Nicholas Pitt, Powered by Light / Alan Spencer, James Quine,
Scenics & Science, GEORGE AND MONSERRATE SCHWARTZ, STOCKFOLIO, Kirk
Treakle, David Wall, Zone)

Library of Congress Cataloging-in-Publication Data

Champion, Neil.
Temperate woodlands / by Neil Champion.
p. cm. — (Caring for the planet)
ISBN-13 : 978-1-58340-509-3
1. Forests and forestry—Juvenile literature. 2. Forest ecology—Juvenile literature.
I. Title. II. Series.

SD376.C49 2005
577.3—dc22   2004052517

First Edition

9 8 7 6 5 4 3 2 1

Contents

Earth is an amazing place. It is complex, beautiful, and awe-inspiring. There has been life on it for some three and a half billion years. In all that time, it has grown more complex as life-forms **evolved**. Today, there are more species of plants and animals—about 10 million according to one scientific estimate—and more **habitats** in which they live than at any point in Earth's long history. This is our inheritance. It is this that we are changing at a faster rate than ever before. Our ability to alter the environment to suit our own purposes has never been greater. This allows many of us to live longer, more active lives, which is a positive thing. However, there are sides to our development and expansion that are not so positive for the planet.

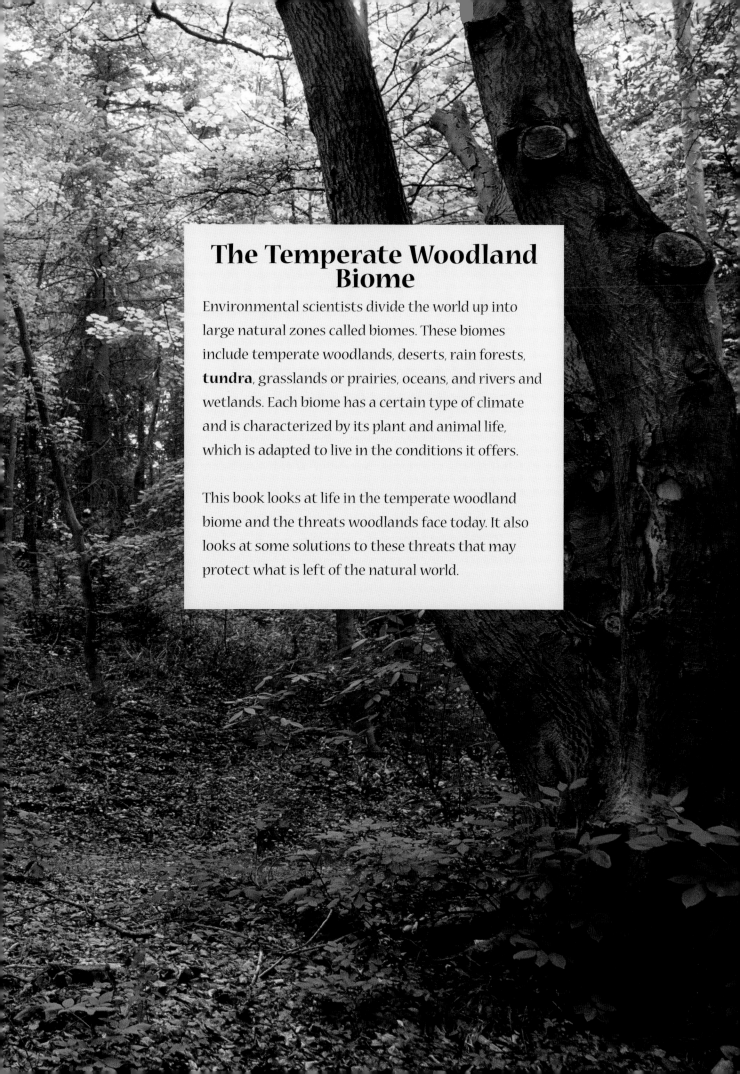

The Temperate Woodland Biome

Environmental scientists divide the world up into large natural zones called biomes. These biomes include temperate woodlands, deserts, rain forests, **tundra**, grasslands or prairies, oceans, and rivers and wetlands. Each biome has a certain type of climate and is characterized by its plant and animal life, which is adapted to live in the conditions it offers.

This book looks at life in the temperate woodland biome and the threats woodlands face today. It also looks at some solutions to these threats that may protect what is left of the natural world.

What Are Temperate Woodlands?

The clue to what makes temperate woodland regions different from other regions on Earth lies in the name. Temperate refers to a type of climate: one that is warm in the summer, cool in the winter, and has two other seasons that mark a change between these—fall and spring. Rain occurs frequently throughout the year (but mainly in fall and winter). The average type of tree growing in the temperate forest needs at least 12 inches (30 cm) of rain a year. Temperate areas lie halfway between the hot and humid equator and the cold and dry poles. In fact, this is what the word temperate means—somewhere in between hot and cold.

Coping with Seasons

All type of trees and plants that grow in an area are dependent on the temperature and the rainfall in that area. They have adapted over time to the conditions of the area. Temperate forests have evolved to cope with the changes in season and to survive the cool and frosty winter, which might include snow and little sunlight for a couple of months each year, along with temperatures that sometimes drop below freezing. Most temperate forest trees shut down for the winter. They shed their leaves and stop growing. Once spring comes around again, they wake up and become active. They put out new leaves and start to make food and grow again. The growing season needs to be at least four months long and is often longer. The trees need this growing time to enable them to cope with the **dormant** winter months.

Fertile Farmland

Woods on the edge of farmland. Temperate woodlands are found where the climate and the soil support human habitation.

Woodland in Winter

A winter scene in a temperate woodland—snow on bare branches and the ground (previous page).

Trouble for Trees

The regions where temperate woodlands grow tend to make excellent homes for people, too. The climate suits humans very well, being neither too hot nor too cold and having plenty of rainfall. This has led to high levels of population density in Europe, North America, Japan, and parts of China. This, in turn, has created problems for the forests over many thousands of years. It is the main reason why the area that temperate woodlands cover has been so greatly reduced over time—people have lived alongside and in the forests, using them as a resource and removing them to make way for their animals, crops, and farms.

Broad-leaved Trees

Most trees in temperate woodlands are broad-leaved. This means that they have large leaves, useful for catching lots of sunlight to turn into food and energy through a process called **photosynthesis**. Examples of broad-leaved trees include oak, beech, ash, maple, and sycamore. Most of these trees are also known as deciduous. This means that the trees lose their leaves in the winter. This can happen for two reasons: very dry conditions or a lack of light.

Some trees shed their leaves to save water. Trees lose water through **transpiration**, part of the process that provides the tree with food to grow and reproduce. When water is scarce, trees stop growing and reproducing, turning to survival mode instead. Shedding their leaves is part of this process. In most temperate forests, however, dry conditions are not usually a problem. Rainfall occurs year-round, although more falls in some months than in others. But winter brings short days and long, dark nights. In the winter, deciduous trees stop growing and lose their leaves to conserve energy, as there is little sunlight to enable photosynthesis to take place. Leaves start to grow back again when winter starts to lose its grip on the forests. Their growth is triggered by longer days, which provide more sunlight.

Amazing Leaves

Leaves are the powerhouses of a tree. Their main role is to assist in food production and **respiration**—in other words, the life-giving functions of the tree. Leaves catch sunlight, which is a form of energy, and use it to help change carbon dioxide from the

Woodland in Fall

The fall season turns the leaves of the deciduous trees in temperate woodlands many colors.

Leaf Fall
Fallen leaves showing all of the colors remaining once the dominant green of chlorophyll has been absorbed back into the tree in preparation for winter.

Why Do Leaves Change Color and Drop Off in the Fall?

The leaves on most trees in a temperate forest turn yellow, red, or brown in the autumn and finally fall off. The color change is due to the fact that the tree removes the green chlorophyll from its leaves, absorbing the chemical into its branches for use again when spring and the new growing season come around. The beautiful colors left behind have always been in the leaves but were hidden by the more dominant green. If leaves stayed on the tree throughout the winter, they might freeze and become damaged. So after they change color, they fall off. The tree produces a leaf scar to heal the wound where the leaf fell off. This helps to protect the tree from disease.

atmosphere into carbohydrates (food for the tree) and oxygen. Most leaves are green because they contain **chlorophyll**, a chemical that helps make carbohydrates.

Leaves on a full-grown tree in the summer overlap to cover a huge area. In fact, the area covered by the leaves can be up to 10 times that covered by the shadow of the tree on the ground. All of this foliage is called the crown. Like a solar panel, the broad, flat area of the leaves is designed to capture all of the sunlight available.

Evergreen Trees
Temperate forests also contain evergreen trees, such as yew, holly, and pine. These trees have found a different way of coping with

the temperate climate, especially in the frosty winter. Instead of losing their leaves, they hang on to them. Because the leaves of these trees are tough and thick, they can resist being frozen and damaged in the winter months. This means that they can produce food year-round, although production from November to March in the northern hemisphere slows down due to the lack of sunlight. These trees can also resist the drought that often occurs when the landscape becomes frozen for periods of time.

Hardwoods and Softwoods

The terms "hardwood" and "softwood" are frequently used when talking about trees. Hardwood trees are mainly deciduous— oaks, beeches, maples, and hickory. They are slow growing, and therefore the wood they produce is dense and very durable. Softwood trees are **coniferous**. They grow quickly, producing light and soft wood. Softwood trees have long been favored by commercial foresters because they can be harvested relatively quickly and sold for fast profits. However, their wood is not of as high a quality as hardwood.

Giant Redwoods

A redwood forest near the town of Rotorua, Bay of Plenty, on the North Island of New Zealand.

Where Temperate Forests Are Found

Temperate forests grow mainly in the northern hemisphere—in Europe, eastern North America, and eastern Asia (including Japan)—in the temperate climatic zone between the Tropic of Cancer and the Arctic Circle. However, special types of temperate forests also grow in the southern hemisphere. In New Zealand and on the island of Tasmania, for example, there are temperate evergreen rain forests. Although the climate is temperate, there are none of the winter frosts or snows that are typical of northern temperate regions. The winters are wet instead, which means trees can grow year-round. The leaves of these trees do not need to fall off in the fall in order for the trees to survive. In south Australia, there are evergreen temperate forests that have to survive drought in the summer. The trees manage this by having evolved leaves that are tough and thick and that do not easily lose water through **evaporation**. In Chile in South America, there is also a small region of temperate forest in the far south.

Europe

Temperate woodlands once covered Europe, except in the cold far north and the hot and dry Mediterranean region. Today, the woodland is extremely fragmented due to heavy exploitation. The main

environmental problem has been associated with thousands of years of human population growth, which has slowly led to the clearing of the landscape of trees. Europe is a heavily industrialized part of the world, which means that pollution also plays a part in forest loss. For example, in parts of eastern Europe, acid rain has badly affected some forests. There are still some large areas of forest left, but most have been cut down and reduced to small patches across an intensively farmed man-made landscape. What is left is well maintained and cared for.

Eastern North America

Once stretching the length of the eastern United States and up into Canada, the great forests have been cut down progressively since the arrival of European settlers in the 17th century. However, there are still large forests in places such as the Appalachian Mountains, and protected areas such as the Great Smoky Mountains National Park help to preserve what remains of them.

Woodland in Spring

Spring bluebells carpet the ground in this deciduous forest in England. Woodlands of this type are characterized by plenty of ground vegetation.

Japan

Japan is another densely populated and industrialized region of the world where temperate forests have suffered from exploitation. However, it is a country of more than 3,000 islands, some of which remain wild and still have extensive forest cover. It is also a mountainous country, which has helped to preserve pockets of old temperate forest.

Eastern China and Korea

These regions have seen serious loss of temperate forest cover, similar to that in Europe. China has a huge population to feed, and most of the low-lying, once forested land has been turned over to agriculture. China destroyed large areas of forest very quickly when the **communist** government announced the "Great Leap Forward," a program aimed at industrializing the country, in the late 1950s. Millions of trees were cut down to fuel furnaces to make iron. The result was an **ecological** disaster. Extensive erosion has now occurred because the trees are no longer there

Japanese Woodland

A temple with a backdrop of mixed woodland in Kyoto, Japan. Kyoto is a city of more than one and a half million people, once the capital of Japan.

to bind the soil together. The loss of trees to support the soil and soak up water has also led to an increase in floods along the banks of the great rivers, such as the Yellow River. In 1991, for example, almost half of China was affected by floods, in which six million people were left homeless.

Southeast Australia and Tasmania

Temperate rain forests thrive in this part of the world. Because of their isolation and climate, they have produced unique plants and animals. The most characteristic trees of these forests are the myrtle beech, Huon pine, and King Billy pine. The Huon pine can live up to 2,000 years. The forests are recognized by the United Nations, and areas have been given **World Heritage Site** status to protect them from exploitation. However, for more than 100 years before this status was gained, these forests were exploited by European settlers, who cleared the trees to grow crops and graze animals. And the regions outside the protected boundaries are still heavily exploited today.

New Zealand

This is an isolated part of the world, with unique species of trees and birds. However, New Zealand's temperate rain forests have suffered over the years at the hands of people. **Maoris** cleared forestland for farming, and settlers from Europe continued the process. Wild and remote areas still contain large, pristine areas of woodland. Introduced species of animals (such as deer, rats, sparrows, and blackbirds) and plants have caused problems in some areas, such as the wilderness area of Fiordland in the far southwest corner of the South Island. Eleven species of birds have become extinct in the region since the early 19th century.

Remote Rain Forest

Pockets of remote and untouched temperate rain forest can still be found in parts of the Patagonian region of Chile and Argentina.

Southern Chile

This isolated area of temperate woodland in the southwest corner of the South American continent has been well-preserved. This is mainly due to the fact that it is far from big centers of human habitation and therefore has not been exploited nearly as much as the woodlands in other parts of the world.

Why Temperate Forests Are Important

Temperate forests are made up of some of the world's most familiar trees—oak, beech, birch, maple, sycamore, and hickory, for example—and are home to some of the best-loved animals—squirrels, bears, foxes, badgers, and numerous bird species. They are among the richest habitats in the world. In the U.S. alone, temperate forests are home to more than 100 species of trees. These, in turn, support a great variety of plants and animals.

Trees as Homes

Trees truly are the skyscrapers of nature, with animals living at all of the different levels, from under the roots up to the highest branches in the crown of the tree. A full-grown tree in the forest provides a home for hundreds of different animals. Insects live beneath the bark, and birds of all kinds nest in the branches or in holes in the tree's trunk. Mammals such as squirrels also take advantage of these towering structures for constructing their **dreys**.

Predators, such as wolves, stoats, and pine martens, use the cover of the forest to hunt for prey. Bears, now rare, still live in a few pockets of isolated woods in North America, remote parts of Europe, and Asia. Deer are still a common sight in many forests, using the dappled light and foliage as camouflage for themselves and their young.

Forest Homes

Red squirrels are found mostly in coniferous forests, but they also live in deciduous woodlands. They build their homes in conifer trees and feed mainly off seeds from the cones.

Most trees in a temperate forest are slow-growing. They can take well over 100 years to reach their full height and may live for several hundred years after this. This means that each individual tree has an important role to play in the life and health of the forest. Over many autumns, their leaves fall. These are recycled into the soil by decomposers such as fungi, beetles, earthworms, and bacteria. This process results in fertile soil in which an abundance of other plants and small trees can grow.

Trees and Climate

Trees have a crucial role to play in regulating the climate, both locally and on a global scale. They help clean the air and keep life-giving water in circulation through a process known as the **water cycle**. They absorb and use both water and carbon dioxide from the atmosphere. Carbon dioxide is one of the major **greenhouse gases** that some scientists believe are contributing to **global warming**. Trees take in this gas and lock the **carbon** inside their growing trunks and branches. They only release it again when they finally die and decompose on the forest floor. Thus, the more trees that grow, the less carbon dioxide there is in the atmosphere to contribute to global warming. Trees also produce oxygen, which is vital for all animals and people to breathe, and in the process help to maintain a balance between the various gases in the atmosphere. They keep the oxygen content in the air stable, at around 21 percent, helping to make life possible—if this were to vary a few percent one way or the other, life on Earth would cease to exist.

Protected Forests

Brown bears in Katmai National Park in southern Alaska. This is a protected region known for its forests and for rivers rich in salmon, which the bears feed upon.

Worldwide, tree cover has been reduced dramatically in almost every country. The effects on climate are difficult to gauge, but by reducing the number of trees worldwide, humans have created the potential for profound changes. Certainly, many scientists now believe that the world is becoming warmer. It seems logical that the reduction in the number of trees is one factor in this complex picture.

Trees and the Landscape

Trees are also important to the landscape. Their roots bind the soil in place, holding it together. This is important in areas exposed to high wind and rainfall, especially where the land is steep, such as in mountainous regions. Heavy rains carry exposed soil downhill much more easily if the trees are no longer there to hold it together. Erosion of this sort is very common in the high mountain regions of the world. In the Himalayas, for example, roads that wind through high passes constantly suffer from landslides and have to be cleared every year after the **monsoon** rains have gone, which is very costly.

Eroded Landscapes

Coastal erosion at Robin Hood's Bay in northeastern England. Erosion is a natural phenomenon, but it occurs at an increased rate once tree cover and other vegetation are removed from the landscape.

Trees also act as windbreaks, preventing wind in flat landscapes from removing the fertile topsoil. This is why stands of trees and hedges are so important in agricultural regions where crops such as wheat and corn are grown.

Wood

Wood from temperate forests has been used by people for thousands of years—to make tools and weapons, build shelters, supply fuel for fires, and build boats and ships, carts and wagons. It is the main ingredient in paper manufacture. Wood also supplies people with oils for making soap and glue, resins for preserving things, and a substance called **cellulose** that can be turned into rayon, a man-made fiber used to make textiles.

Forest Industry

Industrial logging in Tasmania, Australia. When timber plantations are managed carefully, with a policy of replacing felled trees with new growth, the environmental cost can be kept to a minimum.

Threats to Woodlands

The threats to temperate woodlands are not the same everywhere around the world, nor have they remained the same throughout history. However, they all share one thing in common: they come from human activity of one sort or another. This activity started in earnest in Europe around 8,000 years ago, when Stone Age people cleared small areas for their crops and animals using elementary tools, and it continues to the present day. All temperate zones have suffered the same fate.

In fact, the temperate forest is the biome that has been reduced in size more than any other biome on Earth. About 8,000 years ago, trees covered almost half of Earth's surface. Today, this has been reduced by 80 percent. In many countries, woodlands have been reduced to less than 10 percent of their original cover.

There are simple reasons why people have chopped down temperate forests so ruthlessly. Trees grow on fertile soil, which is useful to humans for growing crops and grazing animals. Wood has also always been a valuable resource to humans. People have used too much of it and replaced too little. This is especially true of trees that grow very slowly, such as beech, oak, ash, maple, and yew, typical trees of the temperate forest.

Unfortunately, when temperate forests are cut down, the animals and plants that depend on them also decline. In southeastern Australia, for example, some of the country's most threatened animals and birds are found in the temperate forests. These forests have been almost completely

Forest Fungus

Fungal growth on the trunk of an old tree in an ancient woodland. Temperate forests of any significant age have become scarce in the developed worlds of North America and Europe.

destroyed in the past 100 years. Only a little more than 10 percent of the original forest cover remains due to logging, firewood collection, and clearing for farmland and cattle grazing.

Land Clearing

Southeast Australia isn't the only place where temperate forests have been cleared. In the counties of England and the states of the eastern and southern U.S., temperate forests have been all but removed from sight. The invention of the ax and the plow, probably by the Sumerians (the world's earliest civilization dating from about 3500 B.C.), revolutionized farming. Trees could be felled quickly. Animal power could be harnessed and large areas of soil turned over for sowing wheat, corn, barley, and other crops. As time went by, more land was cleared for the expanding populations. Entire landscapes changed beyond recognition.

The sides of hills in Britain were once clothed in trees, and the fertile valleys were dense with forest growth. Thousands of years of tree felling—to clear land for farming and to harvest wood— have removed most of the cover. Starting in the 17th century in the southern U.S., the land was cleared of oak, beech, and maple trees to grow cotton and other crops, which eventually exhausted the soil. When the Civil War brought slavery to an end in 1865, the cotton industry became uneconomic. The land was returned to the trees, but only pine trees could flourish in the impoverished soil left behind. In China, the process of **deforestation** was well underway by 2000 B.C. Huge areas were cleared of woodland so that people could get at the very fertile soil, called loess, to farm it. The price that was paid came in the form of soil erosion. Because

Fast-growing Conifers

Native deciduous woodlands have been replaced with faster-growing coniferous trees on the sides of these hills in Snowdonia National Park in northern Wales.

of its fine texture, and without trees and their binding roots to protect it, the loess was easily blown away on the wind. The land became less fertile, leading to famine.

The Arrival of the Ax

Stone Age people in Europe and the Middle East some 8,000 years ago probably first used the ax. Before this time, they had been using sharpened flints as tools. An ax was made when someone thought of adding a handle to the stone. This made an efficient cutting tool. An experiment carried out in the 1960s proved the ax's efficiency. Three men cleared trees from 720 square yards (600 sq m) of land in 4 hours using replica stone axes. A whole Stone Age tribe could have cleared a forest in a matter of days. When metal replaced stone in early people's technology, the process became even faster. Iron ax heads were used from about 1000 B.C. in Europe.

Conifer Crop

Stands of commercially grown coniferous trees have been planted as a crop in North Carolina. Native deciduous trees can be seen in the background of this photograph.

Growing Trees for Logs

The use of machinery has helped mechanize the process of logging, allowing more trees to be felled, stripped, and sawed up. This saw mill is on Vancouver Island, Canada.

Logging

Logging is a major industry in some parts of the world. Millions of trees are cut down every day to meet people's needs. Hardwood trees found in temperate forests have always been of use and value. The wood of beech, oak, hickory, maple, ironbark, and other hardwoods has been used in making homes, furniture, fences, and more. However, hardwoods take a long time to grow to maturity—the oak, for example, takes more than 100 years to be fully grown. Softwood coniferous trees such as pine, on the other hand, might be ready to cut down and use in 20 years.

As the natural supply of hardwoods has been exhausted in many areas, these trees have often been replaced with quicker growing softwood trees. These trees are grown in managed forests, in which they are treated like any other crop. They are planted in monoculture stands—huge swaths that consist of only one type of tree—and when they reach a certain height, they are harvested.

Example of the Cork Oak

*About 80 percent of cork comes from trees grown in Portugal and parts of Spain. Most of this product goes to the wine industry. For hundreds of years, bottles of wine have been sealed with cork. It is an ideal material for the job, being light and compressible. However, today cork use is threatened by other materials—plastic corks have become popular and are cheaper to produce, as are screw tops made from metal. This means that the livelihood of the farmers who manage the cork oak trees is under threat. If farmers can no longer make a living from cork, they will have to replace cork trees with something else. So the great managed cork oak forests of Portugal may eventually disappear because of plastic. Plastic is not as **biodegradable** as a natural product such as cork, which makes it more harmful to the environment.*

Grown for Bark

A single cork oak tree on a plantation in Portugal. The bark is carefully stripped to harvest the cork without harming the tree, a process that has been used for hundreds of years.

The crop is then replaced with new trees that will be harvested at some time in the future. While this results in a **sustainable** forest, it also changes the ecology of the area. The plants, shrubs, birds, and animals that have evolved in oak, beech, and maple forests cannot adapt to the new pine forests and die out.

Mineral Extraction and Mining

Where coal, gas, and minerals are found beneath the earth, mining companies are often allowed to remove whatever they need to on the surface to get at the wealth below. This includes trees. To run a mine successfully, roads and houses also need to be built, which involves further clearing of woodlands. Once this happens, the way is open for farmers to move in and start opening up more land.

Collecting Firewood

For thousands of years, people have used firewood to keep warm and cook their food. Today, modern developed countries have largely replaced wood with electricity and gas for most of these needs. However, developing nations in Africa, South America, and Asia still use wood in this traditional way. Over generations of collecting on a small scale, huge areas of countryside have become bare of trees. Many people today have to walk miles to gather even a small number of twigs and branches. In mountainous countries such as Nepal and Peru, bare hillsides have been badly eroded because the trees that once covered them are gone. Devastating landslides have resulted, causing considerable damage to communities.

Pollution

Man-made pollution has become a more recent threat to the health of temperate woodlands. It has grown out of the **Industrial Revolution** that started in Britain in the late 18th century and took off in Europe and the U.S. in the mid-19th century, and in Japan and China in the 20th century. Industry, along with exhaust fumes from cars, trucks, and airplanes, accounts for most of the harmful gases in the atmosphere. These have either had a direct effect on trees (as in the case of acid rain destroying their foliage) or an indirect effect (as in the case of global warming). Logging, mining, and other forest-based industries also produce inevitable levels of pollution. This pollution gets into rivers and soil, and as a result, not only is the land deprived of trees, but fish and other wildlife also suffer from contamination.

Habitat Fragmentation

Habitat fragmentation occurs when parts of a woodland are cleared. The landscape becomes dotted with small patches of trees. This may leave the impression that the woods are still there and are still healthy. But to remain in good condition and sustain the birds, animals, and plants associated with temperate woodlands, the woods have to be of a reasonable size. Species start to become vulnerable or even endangered if they cannot get enough food from their habitat or if their territory is too small to allow their population to grow or remain stable. Fragmented woodlands prevent animal communities from reaching each other, leaving the animals isolated. This problem has affected well-known animals such as the koala in the eucalyptus forests of Australia and the giant panda in the bamboo forests of China.

Dense Foliage
The dense temperate rain forest environment, with eucalyptus and gum trees.

Acid Rain

Acid rain is made when industries put sulfur particles into the atmosphere. Sulfur mixes very easily with rainwater to form a weak acid, called sulfuric acid. This is acid rain. Acid rain damages trees in two ways. It can attack the soil around the tree roots, dissolving nutrients and making the soil toxic. It also attacks the leaves or needles of the tree, turning them brown and making them fall off early. Both of these things mean that the trees get far less in the way of nutrients than they should. At best, this stunts the tree's growth. At worst, it kills the tree.

*Acid rain can be blown hundreds of miles from the source of the pollution and fall on wild areas. The forests of Norway and Sweden, for example, have suffered in the past from acid rain created in the industrial areas of Britain. The **prevailing winds** blow from west to east and carry the harmful substances across the North Sea, where they fall on an otherwise relatively unpolluted landscape. The same is true of parts of the American East Coast, where industrial pollution from Midwestern cities plays a part.*

Deadly Acid

Acid rain has devastated this forest in North Carolina. Leaves have been killed, which in turn has killed the trees.

Extinction Debt

Extinction debt refers to a disturbing event that can happen in woodlands that have been reduced in size. The woods can seem to be in healthy condition, as can the mammal, reptile, and bird populations living there. Although their habitat has been reduced by the loss of trees, plants and animals give the impression of having adapted to the loss. It may look as if the trees that have been removed have made little difference to the overall health of the habitat. Endangerment, or even extinction, is often delayed, and the real cost takes several years—up to 20—after the event to show. Then, the loss suddenly catches up with the ecosystem, causing the communities of plants and animals to drop in population and health. But by that time, it is far too late to do much about it.

Flooding and Hydroelectric Projects

Hydroelectric projects often involve building dams and flooding the landscape behind them. This poses a major threat to temperate forest regions, which are found in areas of high rainfall—up to 20 feet (6 m) every year in places such as Fiordland in New Zealand, one of the wettest places on Earth.

Damaged Landscape

The ugly scar left behind by loggers who have cleared a patch of woodland. This can have the effect of fragmenting the habitat and weakening its ecological integrity.

The combination of rivers and mountains can provide the ideal opportunity to build dams, flood stretches of land behind the dams, and control the water flow to generate power in the form of electricity. However, the flooding destroys large tracts of natural forests, along with all of their plants, some animals, and the homes of birds in the area. Some plant and tree species in New Zealand, for example, have become rare or have even been eradicated on the mainland due to flooding caused by hydroelectric projects. Small islands have been the only refuge for these endangered species. Were the area to be flooded even further, the islands would disappear forever, as would the trees and plants living on them. Fortunately, in the 1960s, a plan to increase hydroelectric power to an existing power station on the South Island of New Zealand by raising the level Lake Manapouri by about 100 feet (30 m) was halted due to public pressure. It was recognized that raising the water level would cause precious and unique island habitats containing rare **orchids** and **podocarp** to be drowned. Since 1990, the area has been protected as a World Heritage Site. It is also part of Fiordland National Park.

National Park

Lake Manapouri on South Island, New Zealand, is situated in the Fiordland National Park. In the 1960s, people all over the country protested plans to flood the region, which would have destroyed its ecosystem.

Overcoming the Problems

When human populations were small, felling trees to meet basic needs did not present a problem for the environment. The rate at which people took from nature was matched by nature's ability to replace the small losses. This is an example of sustainable development. Both sides of the equation were kept in balance—human needs were met, but the stock of trees was also maintained.

However, as human communities grew and people changed from **nomadic** wandering to settled farming, the need for wood increased considerably. Where all of the key resources—water, fertile soil, a warm or temperate climate, and good tree cover—were found in abundance, civilizations developed rapidly. As the people in these civilizations became wealthier and more inventive, they made technological discoveries—for example, how to make better tools and weapons and how to build carts with wheels—and a greater strain was put upon woodlands to cope with the growing demands for raw materials. In addition, trees took up the land that people wanted to farm. As a result, more and more trees were cut down, without regard for the effect of their loss on the environment.

The Modern Plight

The difference today is that we are more aware of the effects that our own needs have on the environment. We have also seen what happens if we don't act to protect the landscape. We have seen vast areas become desert because we have removed the trees and other plants that helped to hold the soil in place. We have seen mountainsides become unstable and collapse because the trees, with their large, binding roots that held the steep slopes together, have been cut down for firewood over generations. We are in the middle of trying to understand why our climate is changing and what part the slow clearing of trees from our landscape might play in this.

Putting Up a Fight

There are many stories from around the world of people putting up resistance to help defend woodlands from further development and degradation. In New South Wales in southeastern Australia, for example, a company made plans to build a charcoal plant in the region of two very important temperate state forests. The plant would have taken about 220,000 tons (200,000 t) of timber out of the Pilliga and Goonoo woodlands to make into charcoal. However, the business never got off the ground. It was stopped in its tracks by the combined efforts of people from the local communities, local councils, and nationwide environmental groups. Their hard work and commitment to stopping the program showed that concerned and sincere people can make a difference in the fight to save the environment.

National Reserves and Parks

The U.S. led the way well over 100 years ago when Yellowstone became the first national park in the world. Other countries have followed. In Britain, the Peak District, Lake District, and Snowdonia all became national parks following an act of Parliament in 1949. Today, there are hundreds of national parks and wilderness and wildlife reserves in temperate forest regions. Parks give some measure of protection to the landscape inside their boundaries. Wild places are preserved from further development or inappropriate exploitation. Nature reserves give even more protection. Rangers keep poachers and hunters out. They look after the trees, felling them when needed to allow for new growth in the forests.

Protecting our Heritage

World Heritage Sites are bestowed by UNESCO (the United Nations Educational, Scientific, and Cultural Organization) in recognition of international importance. This is one such site in northern Sweden.

Protecting Woodland Animals

Habitat destruction and overhunting have been the cause of the decline of many species of animals, especially larger mammals. This includes the bear, wolf, lynx, and bison. Bird species that live in woodlands have also suffered from these twin perils. Today, these animals' last hope of survival lies in strictly protected areas where habitats are preserved, hunters are kept out, and stocks of the animals are bred and distributed more by science than by nature.

Hunted to Extinction

Wolves have been hunted to near-extinction by people in the forests of Europe and North America. This wolf lives in a forest nature reserve in Germany.

Zoos can even play a part. Animals bred in captivity can be introduced back into the wild. Alternatively, animals from areas where the population is healthy can be taken and put into an area where that species once lived but has been eradicated. This has happened with the wolf and the bison in Italy and the U.S. Efforts have been made to reintroduce the wolf to the Highlands of Scotland as well, but so far these have not succeeded. The last wild brown bear was killed in Scotland in the **Middle Ages**. But perhaps one day the brown bear will be returned to this land. However, reintroducing large predatory mammals can meet with strong opposition. For example, a plan to bring the gray wolf back to Yellowstone National Park (put into effect in 1995) was long met with many "no" votes. Farmers feared that the wolves would take their animals, which are their livelihood.

Tourism

The tourist industry worldwide is worth billions of dollars. Every year, big companies advertise beautiful places around the world and offer to take us to them. Every sort of vacation is offered— city-based and cultural, lazing on a hot beach, adventurous and wild, based on board a ship cruising the world. There are even vacations for **eco-tourists**, those who are concerned about the planet and the impact humans have on it.

The Example of Tasmania

Tasmania, an island off the southeast coast of Australia, still has vast tracts of untouched wilderness and some species of animals that are found nowhere else on Earth, such as the Tasmanian devil. Much of this wilderness is temperate rain forest and mountains. It is a favorite place for hikers and those wanting to get away from modern life. The island has seen some development, mostly by hydroelectric companies. However, compared with other regions, it amounts to very little. This is partly due to geography—the island is isolated. But it is also to the credit of the Australian government and national and international conservation organizations, which, over the years, have campaigned to ensure that Tasmania sees minimum development. For example, although dams for hydroelectric plants have been built on a few sites, a proposal to flood the Gordon and Franklin Rivers to make one large hydroelectric plant was strongly opposed and defeated in the 1970s. Today, much of the wilderness is protected. There are four national parks and several state forests, and the whole wilderness area is now a World Heritage Site. This amounts to more than 4,000 square miles (10,000 sq km) of protected wilderness. There are other wilderness areas of the world in temperate zones, but most are not as well looked after and protected as this wonderful island.

Tasmanian Devil

The Tasmanian devil, a carnivorous marsupial found only on this island, lives in the temperate rain forests and hunts at night. It has been adopted as the symbol of the Tasmanian National Parks and Wildlife Services.

Benefits from Tourism

Tourists walking in the Parque Nacional Alerce Andino in Chile. The temperate rain forest trees here have been protected since the park was founded in 1976.

Last of the Herds

Wild bison roam the primeval forest of Bialowieza on the Polish-Byelorussian border (opposite).

The environment can benefit from this situation. Tourists like to get away from the towns and cities where they live and work. They generally like to go to less polluted places, where they can see landscapes and wildlife that cannot be seen at home. Wild and extensive temperate forests fit these requirements. This is one way that trees can pay for their existence in a human-dominated world. They can provide areas for recreation and health. Society will help maintain them if it can see a direct benefit. And, of course, such tourism also provides jobs for people in these regions.

New Farming Practices

Agricultural scientists have recently shown that trees can actually help increase the yield of certain crops. Experiments were carried out in which lines of poplars and cherry trees were planted down the side of narrow fields growing commercial crops such as canola, winter wheat, and barley. The trees took water from deeper underground than the crops, so they did not interfere with their growth. In fact, they gave the crops protection from the wind and battering rain, helping to keep the plants from being damaged. In the future, more and more farmers may be planting rows of trees in their fields, doing themselves and the landscape a big favor.

A Very Wild Place

Scientists believe that 8,000 years ago, temperate woodlands covered Europe and Asia. A squirrel may well have been able to travel from Spain to China through the trees without setting a paw on the ground. All of this has gone. What remains is somewhere between 5 and 10 percent of the original cover. Even what remains is mostly managed woodland. There is very little of the original, truly wild forest left today. Along with the grandeur of these early forests, the big predatory mammals are also mostly gone. Bears, wolves, wild boars, and wild cats have seen their woodland habitat dwindle, and they have been hunted to extinction in many areas.

*Today, the Bialowieza Forest is the only truly wild area of temperate forest left in Europe. To get an idea of what most of Europe and Asia looked like clothed in trees 8,000 years ago, this forest is the place to visit. It is found on the eastern border of Poland with Belarus. It is so special that it has been made a **Biosphere Reserve** and World Heritage Site, under the protection of the United Nations. It has never been tamed by people, although it was once a royal hunting reserve.*

Today, plenty of wild animals still roam the area, including wolves, lynx, beavers, elk, and the last remaining group of European bison. The forest attracts thousands of tourists, who come in hopes of seeing the last of the big mammals that once roamed at will through the ancient forests of Europe. Fortunately, this area has a chance of remaining as it is because it brings money to the region in the form of visitors.

What the Future May Hold

The future appears to hold some very good signs for the preservation of the remaining temperate woodlands worldwide. In some places, the area they cover is even increasing. Nature reserves have proven popular and effective in most places. However, there are also signs that our trees are still under threat. Some of these threats come at a local level, from industries and governments that wish to exploit them or clear them for land. In many countries, there are hundreds of small battles being fought all the time over small patches of woodland under threat from building projects or new roads. People have even gone so far as to live for months in the very trees that local businesses or governments want to cut down. Passions have run very high over the issue of just a small patch of temperate forest.

Other threats to temperate forests come on a very large scale—global warming, for example. If the climate changes over the coming years in the way that some scientists predict, then temperate woodlands in some areas could be in for a very hard time. There is real concern that the **Gulf Stream** that brings warm water from Central America up and across to the western shores of Britain and Europe could be affected by the melting of the polar ice caps. All of this fresh water entering the seas around the North Pole could switch the warm current off. If this happened, the coast of Britain would take on a climate more like that of the east coast of Canada, with long, very cold winters in place of the mild, temperate winters it now receives. Temperate forests would not be able to survive these new conditions. Similarly, some scientists think that with the increase in world temperatures, the dry areas of North Africa and around the Mediterranean Sea could start

Rich Habitat

The rotting trunk of an old oak tree provides a fantastic habitat for insects and fungus alike in this deciduous woodland (previous page).

to extend northward into the rest of Europe. Temperate forests would not be able to adapt to or survive the very dry conditions. They would die out. These alarming possibilities show just how fragile the environment is. It can adapt to change over long periods of time, but not to the sudden alterations in rainfall and temperature that scientists are predicting.

A Return to the Past

When economic habits change among communities, there can often be a benefit for the natural world. On the eastern coast of the U.S., for example, areas that were once farmed have returned to wild woodlands. This is because of the growth of towns and cities in the 19th century in states such as West Virginia and Massachusetts. As people left their farms and homes in search of greater wealth in urban areas, trees and plants grew back and reclaimed the land.

However, change has also worked against the natural world. Throughout the Middle Ages and up to the time of the Industrial Revolution, trees were so important to the people of Britain that they were looked after and managed. To harvest them, foresters

Rural Woodland

This rural scene in Vermont portrays human settlement in a heavily wooded area.

would coppice young trees. This meant cutting back the trunk and branches of the trees. Lots of branches would then grow out of the low trunk, and these could be cut off to be used without killing the tree. There was an endless supply of wood coming out of managed coppiced woodlands all over country, used to make charcoal, to burn on fires, and to build houses. This practice went on for hundreds of years, ensuring that the woodlands would not shrink. They were too economically important for the country to allow that to happen, and they could be exploited in a sustainable manner. However, new technology developed during the Industrial Revolution meant that new sources of power were needed. Coal became the main source, taking over from wood. It fired the boilers of the new industries and was burned to power the new steam trains. **Coal gas** was extracted to give gas lighting. Trees were no longer needed in the same way that they once had been, and the relationship between small rural communities and their forests changed. Once the woodlands lost their economic viability, they became vulnerable. People didn't need them anymore, so many were once more put to the ax to clear more land for farming in order to make money off of the land.

Traditional Woodlands

Managed woodlands have been a feature of countries like England for hundreds of years. Hazel and oak were looked after by people because they were valuable materials used in buildings, ship-making and tools.

Conservation Organizations

Today, there are many organizations, both national and international, that monitor life in fragile and endangered habitats around the world, including temperate woodlands. Their goal is to help preserve these environments long into the future. Here are some of the more well-known organizations:

- **Friends of the Earth**   www.foe.org
Founded in 1971 in Britain, Friends of the Earth is now one of the world's best-known and most respected environmental pressure groups.
- **World Wide Fund for Nature (WWF)**   www.panda.org
Founded in 1961, this Swiss-based organization raises money to fund conservation operations around the world, focusing in particular on endangered animals.
- **Greenpeace**   www.greenpeace.org/usa/
Founded in 1971 in Canada, Greenpeace has grown to become one of the world's biggest and most influential environmental pressure groups. It campaigns all over the world on behalf of the environment.
- **International Union for the Conservation of Nature (IUCN)**   www.iucn.org
This organization publishes *The Red Book*, which presents the most comprehensive picture we have today of the state of the planet in terms of threats to species.

What You Can Do to Help

We can all help the temperate woodlands of the world better cope with the growing population and demands of humans. Here are a few ways you can help:

- Make sure the paper you buy and use comes from a source that guarantees sustainable forests. Many products using paper and cardboard will say if the source of wood is sustainable.
- Recycle wood and wood products whenever possible. In fact, recycle all materials (tin, glass, plastic) whenever possible.
- Get involved with helping to take care of a woodland reserve near you. Many of us live within a few miles of small woodland areas open to the public.
- Get involved at school to find out more about the fascinating lives of trees, some of which grow for hundreds or even thousands of years. Imagine what the world was like when a tree now 500 years old was a tiny seedling. A tree that old would

have started to grow as Christopher Columbus left the shores of western Europe to discover the new continent of America.

• Help and support environmental organizations dedicated to protecting woodlands. There are many of them. Fund-raising events and awareness days can be fun to take part in.

• Planting trees is one of the most useful and rewarding events to get involved with. Watch for notices at the local library or through school or environmental organizations that may advertise upcoming tree-planting events.

• In delicate and beautiful natural environments, take nothing but photographs and leave nothing but footprints. That way, you will always leave the wild places that are left on Earth in the same state in which you found them.

Further Reading

Allaby, Michael. *Temperate Forests*. New York: Facts on File, 2006.

Ganeri, Anita. *Forests*. Austin, Tex.: Raintree Steck-Vaughn, 1997.

Parker, Steve. *Wood*. Milwaukee, Wis.: Gareth Stevens, 2002.

Sayre, April Pulley. *Temperate Deciduous Forests*. New York: 21st Century, 1994.

Tompkins, Terry. *Ravaged Temperate Forests*. Milwaukee, Wis.: Gareth Stevens, 1993.

Woodward, John. *Temperate Forests*. Austin, Tex.: Raintree Steck-Vaughn, 2002.

Web sites

Exploring the Environment: Temperate Rain Forest
http://www.cotf.edu/ete/modules/temprain/temprain.html

The Forest Biome
http://www.ucmp.berkeley.edu/glossary/gloss5/biome/forests.html

Forest Stewardship Council
http://www.fscus.org

Temperate Deciduous Forest Biome
http://www.fw.vt.edu/dendro/Forsite/tdfbiome.htm

Temperate Forest Biome
http://oncampus.richmond.edu/academics/education/projects/webunits/biomes/tforest.html

Glossary

Biodegradable   Something that can be broken down by bacteria or fungi. Non-biodegradable substances, such as many plastics and heavy metals, are very difficult to get rid of in an environmentally friendly way.

Biosphere Reserve   An internationally recognized conservation area administered by the United Nations Educational, Scientific, and Cultural Organization (UNESCO).

Carbon   An element found in several forms and in combination with other elements to form compounds; combined with oxygen, it forms carbon dioxide.

Cellulose   A carbohydrate found in plants that makes up their cell walls.

Chlorophyll   A substance found in most plants that makes them green in color. It absorbs the energy from sunlight and makes it available to the plant for the production of carbohydrates.

Coal gas   A gas that is given off when coal is burned out of contact with air. The gas is made up of carbon monoxide, methane, and hydrogen.

Communist   A person who believes in or lives under communism, a political doctrine that prohibits private property.

Coniferous   Describes trees that have thin needles and produce cones. Most are evergreens.

Deforestation   The removal of forests and woodlands, usually by people. Reasons include clearing land for agriculture or industry and timber harvesting.

Dormant   A state in which an organism shuts down its energy use to a bare minimum in order to survive during difficult periods, such as winter or times of drought.

Dreys   Squirrels' nests, built in trees.

Ecological   Relating to the study of living organisms and their relationships with the environment.

Ecosystem   A natural unit of the environment in which all of the plants, animals, and nonliving components depend on each other in complex ways.

Eco-tourists   Tourists who travel with a more sensitive approach to the impact humans have upon the landscapes they visit.

Evaporation   When water is heated and turns into vapor, it is said to have evaporated. Evaporation is part of the water cycle.

Evolution   A theory which claims that all life has come from single-celled forms and has slowly become more complex.

Global warming   The process by which Earth's climate is thought to be getting warmer through an increase in greenhouse gases.

Greenhouse gases   Gases, including carbon dioxide and methane, that trap heat in Earth's atmosphere.

Gulf Stream   A warm ocean current that originates in the Gulf of Mexico, flows north past the east coast of North America, and moves east across the Atlantic around Newfoundland.

Habitats   Parts of an environment that are self-contained, supplying the needs of the organisms that live within them.

Hydroelectric projects   Projects that produce electricity by using the force and energy from moving water, such as a large river that has been dammed.

Industrial Revolution   The movement from an agricultural society to one based on industrial products. This process began in Britain in the mid-18th century and spread to other European countries and the U.S.

Loess   Soil made from clay, sand, and rich vegetable deposits left behind when glaciers retreated.

Maoris   Native people living in New Zealand when the Europeans arrived in the 18th century.

Middle Ages   The period in European history from the fall of the Roman Empire in the 5th century to the start of the Renaissance in the 15th century.

Monsoon   A wind that blows at certain times of the year in regions of southern Asia and brings huge quantities of rain. The regular rainy period in tropical countries is often called the monsoon season.

Nomadic   A term that describes a wandering way of life. Nomadic people traditionally keep animals or follow the migratory paths of wild animals, living off the land and settling only for short periods of time.

Orchids   Flowering plants that grow worldwide. There are about 15,000 species of orchids.

Photosynthesis   The process by which green plants on land and in the oceans turn sunlight and carbon dioxide from the atmosphere into oxygen and food for themselves.

Poachers   People who illegally shoot animals for meat or to sell to other people as trophies.

Podocarp   Evergreen trees that belong to the yew family.

Prevailing winds   A term used to describe the direction from which the winds most commonly blow in a region.

Respiration   The process of breathing.

Sustainable   Something that can be carried out indefinitely into the future.

Transpiration   The process by which water is lost through the leaves of plants and trees due to evaporation.

Tundra   Land close to or inside the Arctic Circle, where the layer of soil just below the surface is permanently frozen due to year-round low temperatures.

Water cycle   The natural cycle in which water evaporates from bodies of water and is given out from plants into the atmosphere, where it eventually condenses again to form clouds and precipitation.

World Heritage Site   A cultural or natural site that is considered to be of outstanding value to humanity. The World Heritage program is administered by UNESCO.

Index

2318756